PARENTING THE PURE ATHLETE

PARENTING THE PURE ATHLETE

HELP YOUR ATHLETE
Maximize Performance
Achieve Their Goals
Build Lasting Character

BRITT LEE

PARENTING THE PURE ATHLETE

Published 2021

Printed in the United States of America

Hardcover ISBN: 978-1-7375655-2-9
Softcover ISBN: 978-1-7375655-0-5
Ebook ISBN: 978-1-7375655-1-2

Library of Congress Control Number: 2021900370

to Kay
my biggest encourager and best friend.
I am so blessed to share life with you.

to Annie, Katherine, Brittain, and Jack
you are my pride and joy,
and I'm so blessed to be your dad.

A pure athlete is one
who is developing into the
best version of themself,
maximizing their potential
in sports and life.

CONTENTS

Part III: SPORTS AND LIFE

Introduction:

WEARING
MANY HATS

Another unexpected loss happened last week. Frustration and discouragement are recurring emotions my son has wrestled with all too often in recent months. As the father of a young athlete, I must set aside my own frustration, quickly switching hats from cheerleader to sports psychologist.

I'm a sports parent and my young athlete needs me. To console him and help him work through his disappointment. To help him see the bigger picture and learn from a difficult experience. To help him move through the negative to see the positive. To help him refocus on his future goal.

Sound familiar? If you are parenting a young athlete who is seriously pursuing their sport, you have likely experienced this scenario at some point. And if not, you will.

Being a sports parent is enjoyable and exhilarating at times. The journey provides amazing opportunities to build a stronger relationship with your kid, but it can also produce significant relational strain. It may produce the financial win of a college scholarship, but it will definitely add stress to the family budget. It offers fantastic opportunities to teach important lessons to your young athlete, but these opportunities will be easily missed if you don't seek them out.

I am blessed to be a parent of four great kids. My two oldest girls are adults now but during their tween and teen years they played multiple sports at a recreational level, while also enjoying a variety of non-sports activities.

My twin boys, however, are sports fanatics. Gifted athletically, they played almost every sport until their teen years, when they each decided to focus on pursuing their goal of playing Division 1 college tennis.

They are now seniors in high school, and we are nearing the end of a sports journey that has been challenging. We have logged countless hours and miles driving to training academies during the week and out-of-town tournaments on weekends. Week after week. Month after month. Year after year.

Like most sports parents, I've worn many hats. Manager and coach. Cheerleader and silent spectator. Psychologist and banker. Encourager and disciplinarian. Nutritionist and trainer. And at all times . . . parent. I would like to report that I've always worn these hats well. But I haven't.

My family will tell you that I've struggled with some of these roles at times. But I've worked hard to do what's best for my athletes. I've observed other parents and sought advice. I've scoured the internet for information and expertise. I've pondered and apologized. I've seized opportunities when possible, and I've prayed a lot. And as we approach the end of the youth sports journey, I'm grateful for all of it. Well, most of it.

Yes, it has been tough. But my boys have learned valuable life skills. We have amazing memories, and the quality time we've spent together has paid lasting dividends in our relationships. It's been a rewarding journey.

I wrote this book for the millions of parents who are already on or about to embark on similar journeys. I don't pretend to have all the answers, but along the way, I often wished I had a resource to prepare me for the twists and turns I would have to navigate, all the hats I would have to wear. I hope this book does that for you.

Part I

THE BIG PICTURE

1

IDENTIFYING
THE WHY

Studies have documented that approximately 18 million kids in the United States, ages 6-12, play a team or individual sport, while only 7.9 million continue playing sports at the high school level. For many of those who continue to play, the athlete and their parents will make a decision during the middle school years that athletics will be a priority in their lives. And in today's high-level, youth sports world, that decision comes with a price tag for everyone involved. That price is not limited to dollars and cents, which can be substantial, but also includes sacrificing time and numerous other activities along the way.

Sounds daunting, I know. And if you are just beginning, it is. Thus, the high-level sports journey should not be entered into lightly. It's exciting, yes, but it's also full of challenges. And during the challenging times, you and your young athlete will need to have a firm grip on why you are doing it.

So, what is your why? And more importantly, what is your athlete's why? Because an investment of this much demands a why.

Defining the why will help inform decisions on what to invest in this process and which other activities should move to the back of the line. The why helps athletes set primary and secondary goals, making decisions easier throughout the journey because the desired destination is already known.

I have seen many families investing similar time and resources for a wide variety of whys. Here are some of the more common ones:

- I want to play on my high school varsity team.
- I want to get an athletic scholarship to college.
- I simply want to play a sport in college.
- I love sports and think it is a healthy area to invest my time in.
- I want to be a professional athlete.

For my boys, the why was pretty simple. From the very beginning, they both dreamed of playing Division 1 college tennis. They never thought beyond that, they simply wanted to be college athletes.

For me, my why was three-fold. First, I wanted to support my boys' dreams of playing in college. And while the thought of an athletic scholarship was enticing to me, I knew the costs of getting there would likely exceed the future scholarship amount. Second, I saw athletics as an area where we could

Big **impact** begins
with a clear **vision**.

spend significant time together, sharing a common interest. Last, but certainly not least, I knew I could leverage their sports experiences to teach valuable life lessons that develop strong character.

These whys influenced the decisions we made throughout the journey. They helped my boys prioritize difficult choices, providing a path for setting weekly and monthly goals to reach their desired destination. The why made skipping a social event to prepare for an upcoming tournament a much easier decision.

Finally, teaching your young athletes to identify the why is an exercise that will help them in many areas, enabling them to align their actions and goals, helping them focus on decisions that will move them in the right direction.

Does your athlete have a why? You may think you know but have you ever had a conversation with them about it? Have you revisited the why lately?

If the answer is no to either of those questions, schedule time together to discuss it. Let them come up with their own why, then review it with them. Teach them to consider the bigger picture before making decisions. They will be better for it. In sports and in life.

2

THE ATHLETE'S COMMITMENT

In the remote chance you haven't heard of him, Tim Tebow is the Heisman Trophy winning quarterback who won two national championships with the Florida Gators. He has loads of talent, no doubt, but he reached the pinnacles of college football success in large part because of his unparalleled commitment and drive to achieve his goals. In his book, *Through My Eyes*, Tebow gives us a glimpse into what real commitment looks like. Even at an early age, Tebow prioritized what he wanted to achieve, and his actions reflected those priorities. Day in and day out. In the trenches. Year after year. I call that "Tebow-level" commitment.

"Tebow-level" commitment is rare. Few young athletes have it. You see, commitment is not about desire, and it's not solely about having the right priorities. Both are involved, for sure, but they aren't the main factors. Rather, real commitment is about consistently giving action to those priorities. It means focusing first on what matters most. Every day.

Maybe this isn't an issue for your athlete, but for most young people, it is. The distractions are constantly tugging at them. Social media and YouTube. Hanging with friends and sleepovers. Attending high school events and playing pickup hoops. Video-gaming. SportsCenter. And the list goes on and on.

Don't get me wrong. These distractions are not inherently bad; in fact, many are positive activities that help them become well-rounded people. But if your athlete is trying to achieve a serious sports goal, these distractions will fight for their time and will test their commitment to achieving their goal.

Ok, let's be honest. Most of us struggle with distractions preventing us from doing what matters most in our lives, don't we? There are many days when my head hits the pillow and I realize that while I was pretty busy all day, I neglected some of the areas that matter most to me. And before falling asleep, I tell myself that tomorrow will be different. Tomorrow, I will exhibit "Tebow-level" commitment!

As I talk with other sports parents, many have young athletes that deal with the commitment issue from time to time, or maybe all the time. The athletes genuinely desire to be the best they can be, but often shortchange the daily training regimen required to achieve their goal.

Unfortunately, there is no silver bullet or secret formula. This is simply an area that requires periodic discussions when you observe your athlete's commitment going south.

Call them check-points. They can take different forms, but here's an example of how you might approach it with your young athlete.

Can you take a few minutes to think about and share with me what you see as the biggest priorities in your life, as well as the smaller priorities, because I want to ensure that I am committing my time and resources to the areas that you are really committed to?"

Once they have finished this exercise, move on to part two . . .

Now, take a look at the last week and how you spent your time. Write it down and be honest.

When they have completed the task, sit down with them and review the results. For most kids, this exercise provides a great opportunity to discover and discuss the gaps between what they are actually investing time in and what they say they are committed to.

My boys and I did this exercise at the end of a week which left me frustrated by their lack of commitment to their sport. The data was hard to argue with—they had been on the court that week for only 8 of the 168 available hours! As a means of comparison, many of their competitors were on the court 3-4 hours per day.

Those facts were pretty eye-opening to them, leading to a productive discussion about the commitment required to achieve their goals. Oh, their goals had not changed. Their stated priorities had not changed. But their actions were not in alignment with either. They were not demonstrating real commitment.

At the end of our discussion, I asked them to create their own weekly plan to demonstrate greater commitment going forward. This was a much better approach than me blowing up about their lack of commitment (I know because I've done that a few times).

For their plan, my boys figured out the number of available hours they had each week (eliminating sleep time, school/study time, eating time), and still ended up with over 50 hours during the week for focusing on both big and small priorities. They were then able to determine the time required to achieve their sports goals and created a plan to make it happen. And guess what? They still had free time for their smaller priorities.

Simple as that! And we have never had an issue with commitment again. Ha. I wish that were true. They still need parental reminders at times. And to be candid, it doesn't always come naturally in my life either. Maybe the same is true for you. If so, remind yourself of that and be patient.

But seize the opportunity to continue teaching them the value of commitment. Remind them that commitment begins with a decision. Then a plan. And then it requires frequent checkpoints to stay on a direct path to the desired destination.

It is true for sports, and it is true for life.

Focus **first**...
on what matters **most**.

3

THE PARENTS' COMMITMENT

I once read that Jason Heyward, an outfielder for the Chicago Cubs, traveled for several hours every day after school to play Little League Baseball in East Cobb, one of the nation's premier development programs for youth baseball. Jason was committed, yes, but you know who really showed commitment—his parents.

Let's be real. Jason didn't drive himself; his parents drove. He didn't pay for the equipment and league fees . . . they did. He didn't pay for tournament fees for travel ball, for hotels, for gas, for food . . . they did. And like you and me, they gladly did it because they loved him and were committed to their athlete and his goals.

In the case of the Heyward family, the return on their investment paid off handsomely, as their son is enjoying a lucrative career as a professional baseball player. For most families, however, a multi-million-dollar contract and professional career are not chapters in their stories.

If your kid is serious about pursuing a high-level sports goal, you will also be required to make a substantial commitment. In the early years, when participation in an individual or team sport is almost a rite of passage for 6-12 year-olds, the parents' commitment is fairly low—getting your kid to a practice or two each week, attending a game, paying league fees, and occasionally providing the refreshments. That's not too burdensome. And the payoff of watching them play, win or lose, is usually very fun at the younger ages. Many parents look forward to this stage and enjoy it immensely.

As the little ones become tweens and then teens, the goals become loftier, as does the parents' commitment in terms of time and money. Yes, there is still much fun to be had and many great experiences to enjoy, but there are also setbacks, disappointments, injuries, travel, decisions, conflicts and substantial expenses. And you, as a sports parent, are in the middle of all of it.

I have been at it for about eight years now, traveling to various states for tournaments, planning schedules, ensuring we have the right coaches, managing equipment needs, researching nutrition, etc, etc.

I am not unique. In fact, I know lots and lots of parents who are doing the same. And one thing many of us have in common is . . . we are weary! When I return home from a weekend tournament on a Sunday evening, you would think I was the one who played all weekend, as I am exhausted, both mentally and physically.

For those of you who already have teenagers pursuing a goal of playing a varsity high school or college sport, there is little for you to learn in this chapter. As you read it, you may simply be responding with a hearty "Amen." But for those of you who are just starting out, or ready to take a step from recreational sports to a more serious level, buckle up for the commitment you will need to make.

But here's the other side of the story. For parents who made the big commitment and are now finished, most miss it. Immensely. You see, the payoff (not financial for most of us) makes it worth it. Great experiences with our athletes, our kids. Memories to last a lifetime. Awesome opportunities to teach life lessons from the experiences on the court, field, track, course, floor, or pool. Enjoyable relationships with other parents. And so much more.

Recently, I watched Dominic Thiem win the U.S. Open Tennis Tournament. It was his first Grand Slam Championship, a huge deal in the tennis world. During his post-match interview, he expressed genuine, heartfelt appreciation for everything his parents had given to make the moment happen. In fact, emotion got the best of him, making it difficult for him to get the words out. But he did. And it was moving.

Thiem is 27 years old, but he hasn't forgotten. And he isn't unique. We have heard many great athletes do the same when they achieve a major goal. In their own words, they acknowledge the incredible commitment their parents made to help them achieve their goals.

We don't know what commitment looked like in each of their cases, but we know it was huge. Just like your commitment to your young athlete is. And whether your athlete reaches the pinnacle of sports success or not, the journey itself will be worth it. So, if you're tired, press on. A day is coming when you will miss it, and you'll be glad you made the commitment.

Athletes commit to the **goal**,
parents commit to
the **journey**.

4

THE PARENTS' GOAL FOR THEIR ATHLETE

Why do parents do it? Why do we turn our lives upside down in the high-level youth sports culture? Why do we spend so much money on coaches, training, equipment, and travel? Why do we invest so much time hauling them around to practices during the week, and then give up our entire weekends for their sports events? Why do we contemplate missing a holiday or using our hard-earned vacation time for one more youth sports tournament? What goal are we pursuing by doing these things?

Have you ever slowed down enough to think about that?

Ideally, our sports parenting goal is simply to help our kids pursue and achieve their dream of playing in high school, college, or even professionally. And thus, the sports-related actions I referenced above reflect this "shared sports goal" we have with our young athletes.

As sports parents, however, we must ensure that our sports goals serve, rather than dominate, our broader parenting goals. We've all seen it, in the movies and in real life, when parents emphasize sports over everything else. When we see it in someone else, it's easy to spot. But how do we recognize when we are overemphasizing a sports goal? Here are some red flags I've learned to recognize in my life . . .

- My conversations with my kid are 75% or more about their sport.
- My sports conversations with my kid are 90% about their performance, rather than what they are learning that helps them develop as people.
- The parenting conversations I have with my spouse are 75% about our kid's sport.
- In my idle time, my thought life is dominated by what I can do to help my kid perform better in their sport.

I would love to report that none of those red flags have ever been raised for me, but the fact-checkers in my family would call me out. The reality is that it's easy to get out of balance.

Back when I was a kid, this was much easier for parents. We didn't have the "all-in" sports culture that exists today. Sure, there was still a level of commitment required, but kids didn't have to play travel ball at 11 years old to make the high school team one day. Kids could play 3-5 sports and compete well at all of them. Sport psychologists, speed and agility trainers, and sports academies were a rarity.

But today's youth sports culture demands more com-

Let's raise productive **people**, not just productive **athletes**.

mitment and more investment for a young athlete to achieve success. And at the levels required, it's easy for parents to focus so much on the sports goal that the broader parenting goals get lost in the shuffle. We must protect ourselves against that, and for me, that requires periodic reassessments to make sure I'm not falling into that trap.

Several years ago, I was talking to a college tennis coach whose son was playing in the same tournament as mine. We were discussing some of the challenges of raising young athletes who were very focused on achieving their sports goals, sometimes to the detriment of other important facets of life. I will never forget the statement that this dad, a college coach, made to me. He said, "My son will leave home soon enough, but for now my job is to raise a well-rounded young man, not just to raise a tennis player."

That stuck with me. It reminds me that my greatest parenting goal is not about athletics. And in my opinion, yours shouldn't be either.

So, as you think about your goal as a sports parent, remember that parenting is the most important job you will ever have. Given that, have you determined your primary parenting goal unrelated to sports? When your kid leaves the nest, what do you hope you have accomplished with them? Does your current parenting reflect that goal?

If you feel uncertain about your answers to those questions, take some time to figure it out, then make adjustments if needed. Make sure the athletic goals effectively serve the broader goals. Make sure that one day your kid won't say, "All my mom or dad cared about was athletics."

5

BALANCING THE NEEDS OF THE FAMILY

Have you ever watched ESPN's *The Book of Manning* documentary? It's one of my favorite episodes from the popular *30 for 30* series, telling the story of Archie and Olivia Manning raising three sons who rise to the upper echelons of football success. As you probably know, Peyton and Eli Manning both became Super Bowl MVP quarterbacks, and Cooper seemed destined for the NFL before an issue with his spine ended his college football career.

Yes, these boys had talent, but as sports parents, Archie and Olivia must have done a lot right for their sons to achieve so much athletic success. And based on what we can see, it appears that these parents instilled solid values in them as well, as they have all become well-respected family men in their own rights.

I imagine that football was a dominant topic in the Manning home, in terms of conversation, focus, and time. Fortunately, even though there were significant age differences among the boys, they all shared a passion for sports and had similar goals. For Archie and Olivia Manning, that had to make balancing all the boys' activities a little easier.

But what if one or two of the Manning boys had not been interested in sports? Sounds funny, I know, but what if Eli's passion had been music? And what if Cooper was into hunting and fishing instead of football? How would those differences have changed the parenting dynamic for the Mannings?

That is the situation many sports parents are in, and it can be super challenging. In fact, if you are parenting a serious athlete and also have kids who aren't pursuing high-level sports, you will likely struggle with balancing your time among them.

Of course, this challenge is not unique to parents of young athletes; in fact, all parents with multiple kids struggle with balance at times. But in my experience, when you add high-level sports into the equation, balance becomes even more difficult for parents to achieve.

Why?

Because today's high-level sports culture is so incredibly demanding if your kid is "all in." Between all the weekend travel and daily chauffeuring, among other requirements, there can be little time left over. And for many parents, who share the love for their kid's sport, it is easy to become unbalanced in the amount of time devoted to your young athlete, as opposed to the rest of the family. That's where the tension comes in.

So, how should sports parents balance the demands of

high-level athletics for one child with their desire and need to be present and involved in the lives of their other kids? How do you ensure that the family is not dominated by the athletic pursuits of ONE of its members?

I have two awesome daughters. My oldest was a music major who now works as a worship leader in a church in another state. Growing up, she played recreational lacrosse, soccer, and tennis, but her primary passion was music and theatre. Her younger sister is a college senior at the University of Georgia, where she is having a great experience both academically and as a Young Life leader. Prior to college, she played softball and tennis, ran cross country and track, and performed in plays.

Like many kids, my girls enjoyed a variety of activities, rather than focusing on one. You can probably sense that I am proud of the young women they have become. But their path was different than that of their younger brothers, whose athletic goals demanded more of my time and energy.

More than once, I hate to admit, one of my girls made a comment that suggested I was too focused on her brothers' sports. My initial response was usually defensive. Sometimes I would try to justify myself by explaining the "requirement" of time I had to give at this level of sports. Sometimes I would just get quiet, frustrated that I was being called out when I was giving so much (just not to them).

But I knew they were right. I was out of balance, even though I tried hard not to be.

Maybe you've been there, or maybe you're there now. You may feel you are giving all you have but are still coming up short when it comes to giving all of your kids the attention they desire. You may wonder how you can do it all, and if so, you are in good company. Parenting is demanding work. Parenting multiple children is even more demanding. And being a sports parent will make it even harder.

So how do we achieve the balance that our families need from us? Well, there are no easy answers. No one has the exact formula, and everyone's family is different. But what all parents have in common is that all our kids need and deserve our time and attention. And they all need to know that each of their lives are important to us.

Making that happen requires intentionality. It requires listening. It requires time. Sometimes it requires stepping away from *something* you love—the sport one of your kids is pursuing—to step toward *someone* you love, who needs your time just as much. You may miss a game or a match, but you won't regret it.

I've been fortunate that both the gentle and stinging reminders my daughters shared with me on occasion, along with my own self-awareness, have been enough to help me maintain healthy relationships with each of my kids. And you can too.

So, don't throw your hands up. Keep listening to all of your kids. Keep making adjustments. Keep striving for balance. It's challenging I know, but in the end, it will be worth it.

Balance is a wonderful place that is difficult to **find** and easy to **lose**.

6

OWNING IT—
THE "MOUNTAINTOP"
OF COMMITMENT

This chapter wasn't in my original plans. But that changed with a text I received today regarding one of my sons. He is currently rehabbing from knee surgery, and the text was from his coach. It went something like this . . .

He has not reached out to me with regards to the jump-roping I mentioned. He's got to initiate these things, can't be me holding his hand. He's got to want this more than you and I want it for him and put in the work necessary to get there.

In other words, he has to OWN IT!

To be clear, my son is committed. He wants to achieve his goal, and he's willing to give up a lot of other stuff to achieve it. And when his coach or I put a plan together for him, he will commit to do it.

But owning it is a different story. It is a different level of commitment; one that doesn't require accountability. Sounds great, I know. But getting a teenager to fully own the achievement of their goals is a pipe dream for most parents.

As the title of this chapter states, that type of ownership is the mountaintop, the summit. And like any summit, it is nice to daydream about . . . seeing my kids research coaches, tournaments, equipment, etc, then bringing the information to me for approval and payment. It would be awesome if I never had to ask them what their practice plan for the coming week looks like or remind them to eat and hydrate well before competition.

But let's be honest, I haven't run across many parents who have achieved that state with their young athletes. If you are one of them, congratulations. Please don't look down on the rest of us.

But if you're a parent that gets frustrated when your athlete doesn't show enough ownership, welcome to the club. Welcome to parenting teenagers.

This past weekend, my wife and I spent several hours discussing the text I received from my son's coach. We talked about what we were doing right and what we could do different to accelerate the development of ownership. Where do we draw the line and stop doing for them? When do we let something important go undone? When do we let them fail? What should our expectation be?

The views at the **summit** of ownership are worth the **journey** to get there.

These are all important questions for parents of athletes, and for parents in general. The answers are not simple. Ownership must be developed over time. It comes with maturity. It's not a light with a simple off to on switch. For most kids, it's more like a light on a dimmer switch that gets brighter a little bit at a time.

As parents, you can accelerate the process with periodic conversations. Use these discussions to point out areas for them to own, then hand them over. Not too many at once, rather, help set them up for success. They may stumble at times, but it will be ok. It's how they learn to own. It's the path to the mountaintop.

7

THE HIGH COST OF SPORTS PARENTING

If you are close to the end of your sports parenting journey, you might want to skip this chapter, because it could be depressing . . . a sobering reminder of how much you have spent on your young athlete's journey over the years. Maybe you've been smart and never added it all up. You've avoided the big total number. But you still have a pretty good sense that the price tag is a big one.

If you are in the early stages of this journey or about to crossover from recreational sports to a higher level, this chapter is for you. Not to discourage you from moving forward, but to help you understand what you are signing up for. So, here is the big idea of this chapter.

Drumroll please.

HIGH LEVEL YOUTH SPORTS ARE COSTLY . . .
FINANCIALLY AND OTHERWISE.

The sport your athlete is pursuing will dictate how much—some sports are more expensive than others—but most are pretty expensive. Here is a list of some of the things you will almost certainly spend significant money on . . .

- Equipment
- Apparel
- Individual Coaching
- Academies (depending on the sport)
- Speed, Agility, Strength Training
- Tournament Fees
- Hotels
- Gas
- Eating Out
- Supplements (legal ones like protein, hydration mixes, etc)
- Gym/Club memberships
- Doctors
- Physical Therapy
- Surgeries
- Nutritionist

At the beginning of my journey, I wouldn't have expected to spend money on each of these categories, and while many sports parents don't hit them all, I have. And it's been a lot. Some of these categories show up in recreational sports, so you may already be used to spending money here. I can assure you though, the cost of equipment and coaching, for example, is significantly higher as you move into higher levels of your sport.

When spending your **time** and **money** on youth sports, think of it as an **investment**.

In addition to monetary costs, you and your athlete must be prepared for other costs. The first is TIME. You know the old saying, "Time is money." Well, if that's true, then the cost of sports parenting is extremely high.

You (at least one parent) and your athlete should be prepared to invest substantial time in your sport. Time spent planning, driving, watching, thinking, discussing, preparing, and on and on.

Here's the good news. If you enjoy your athlete's sport, you will enjoy most of the time you invest in it. And for most parents, if your kid enjoys it, you will learn to enjoy it also.

Here's the best news. The large *quantity* of time you are investing will be *quality* time you are spending with your kid.

In addition to the time spent, there is also time lost. What I mean is that both you and your young athlete will incur what is referred to in business as OPPORTUNITY COSTS, the cost of missing out on another important opportunity. In simple terms, due to the demands of pursuing their sport, your young athlete will miss out on some other good things. For example, their friends may be going to the lake one weekend, but they will miss out because of a tournament or game they have. That may not seem like a big deal, but it will happen frequently to them. They will have to make some tough choices and pass on some good opportunities. And so will you.

So, if you are at the beginning of the journey, you and your young athlete need to be ready for what is in store. High-level youth sports is costly. But for my family, it has been worth it. The return has been great. And it can be for you as well.

8

IS THERE A RETURN ON INVESTMENT IN OUR FUTURE?

I f you live in Atlanta, or if you are a big baseball fan, you probably have heard of Jeff Francoeur. For those of you who haven't, Jeff grew up in Lilburn, Georgia, and he was blessed with loads of athletic talent. His parents were both educators, so I'm sure the cost of being sports parents supporting Jeff's ambitions were significant. Jeff had a storybook high school sports experience, starring on state championship teams in both baseball and football, culminating in a two-sport athletic scholarship to Clemson. This is the big payoff that many sports parents and young athletes are striving for, but Jeff never made it to Clemson. Instead, he was drafted by the Atlanta Braves in the first round, inking a deal that paid a signing bonus in excess of $2,000,000.

For David and Karen Francoeur, Jeff's parents, the college scholarship Jeff earned would have produced a positive ROI for all they invested in his youth sports journey. But when Jeff opted for the multi-million-dollar contract that led to a lucrative major league baseball career, the ultimate dream was realized. Pretty strong return on investment, you might say!

For most sports parents, the Francoeur's story will not be theirs. Only a VERY SMALL percentage of us are raising future professional athletes. And according to the NCAA, only 2% of the 7.8 million high school athletes even earn college athletic scholarships. And most of those only earn partial scholarships. These facts are not intended to discourage you; your young athlete may be among the 2%. But if that's what we sports parents are counting on as a return on our investment, about 98% of us are going to be underwater. We're going to be disappointed. We're going to wonder if it was all worth it.

On the other hand, maybe there are other benefits to be realized. Maybe the ROI is much more than a financial return. Maybe you will look back one day on your large investment of money and time and see amazing non-financial benefits. Such significant benefits that you would encourage other parents to make a similar investment. That's where I am.

As my family approaches the end of our youth sports journey, some college scholarship dollars may still come our way. But even if they don't, our investment has been worth it. Yes, the costs have been high. But the benefits have been amazing. Many of the memories we have built are priceless to me. Numerous weekend trips together. Quality time in the car to talk about both meaningful and meaningless stuff, building

Big **investment**.
Big **returns**.

deeper relationships that will last a lifetime. Wonderful and difficult experiences that provided natural opportunities to walk and talk through important life lessons with my young athletes.

And if those benefits aren't enough, I am also really grateful my boys had something positive to pour themselves into during their middle/high school years. It didn't have to be sports; it could have been something else that produced similar benefits. But for my boys, the high-level youth sports journey was the path.

Like you, I have many friends who are sports parents, navigating similar demands across all different youth sports landscapes. From time to time, most express weariness with the grind and/or some frustration with the high cost of the journey. And then the journey is over. And we miss it. And often, that's when we really take time to reflect on all the benefits we and our young athletes realized along the way.

For my kids and me, the finish line is in sight. I can assure you that I am now fully aware of the costs, and they are more significant than I expected when we began. But I'm also very mindful of the benefits, some already realized, and some yet to come. A significant investment yielding substantial returns. That's a strong buy in my book, and I would recommend it to anyone.

9

LIVING YOUR DREAM THROUGH YOUR ATHLETE

If you have seen the movie *Friday Night Lights*, you will remember a scene where Tim McGraw "loses it" on his high school son. McGraw plays Charles Billingsley, a former star football player who is consumed with his son's performance on the football field. In this particular scene, the elder Billingsley (McGraw) comes on the field during a high school football practice to abuse his son verbally and physically for dropping a pass. As a parent, the scene is difficult to watch. You find yourself hoping that another parent or coach is going to step in and confront the out-of-control parent. But no one does, and eventually the son returns to practice, hurt and humiliated by his father's poor behavior towards him.

Admittedly, this scene is an extreme example of an unbalanced sports parent. But if you've been in youth sports for very long, you've seen some version of that story play out in real life. Hopefully it isn't you (if you aren't sure, ask your spouse and they will tell you). Yes, we all get intense at times, excited at times, and frustrated at times. Sometimes the thrill of victory and the agony of defeat can be almost palpable within us. But at the end of the day, we are helping our kids chase *their* dreams, not our own.

But for some small subset of sports parents, they have crossed over. Their young athlete has become a vehicle to live through in pursuit of their own unfulfilled sports dream, or they are simply consumed with wanting their kid to perform perfectly. For that group of parents, this is a dangerous place to be. Yes, your young athlete/you might win the trophy. They/you might achieve the scholarship and/or big contract. But somewhere along the journey, the relationship will become strained. Resentment will grow into bitterness, ultimately leading to a broken relationship. That's a bleak picture, but it's how the story usually plays out if you don't recognize extreme behavior and make course corrections.

So how do we recognize it? How do we passionately support our young athletes without crossing to the other side?

Well, it begins with self-awareness—taking honest stock of the motivations, actions, and emotions you have when it comes to your athlete's sports performances. How extreme is your reaction when your young athlete under-performs? Are your own desires, emotions, frustrations about your athlete's performances stronger than theirs? Your honest answers

Youth sports should be about the **kids**' dreams, not the **parents**' dreams.

to these questions will tell you a lot about the health of your engagement as a sports parent.

If you still aren't sure, ask someone close to you—your spouse, another family member, or a close friend. If you have crossed over to the unhealthy side of sports parenting, they'll probably be able to tell you right away. In fact, they likely have been wondering how to discuss it with you, and your question will open the door.

Finally, if you find yourself over the line at some point, take action right away. Talk to your young athlete about it and ask forgiveness. Back away for a time to gain perspective and balance. Refocus on the person you want your young athlete to become, rather than what you want them to achieve.

There are many ways to regain a proper perspective. How you do it doesn't matter so much, just find a way to get back to the other side of the line. It might be difficult, but it will be worth it. For you, and more importantly, for your athlete.

Part II

HELPING YOUR ATHLETE SUCCEED

10

CAN I COACH AND PARENT WELL?

I f you have the time, I highly recommend coaching your kids during the early years. I coached mine in many sports when they were really young and had a blast doing it. What little expertise I needed, I drew from my own playing days and from the endless coaching resources available online. But once your young athlete becomes serious about pursuing higher level sports, coaching them yourself may not be the best idea.

For many of you, that is obvious. Your athlete is playing a sport in which you don't have the expertise to help them develop the skills needed to achieve high-level success. For others, however, you have effectively coached your kids through their early years, and the following thoughts are now running through your brain.

- *But I played in college and have the expertise to coach my kid.*
- *But it has worked well so far and the cost of hiring outside coaches is so much.*
- *But it is so convenient, and I have the time in my schedule to do it.*

These are all legitimate considerations and one of them may sway you to continue in the roles of both parent and coach. But keep in mind that they are different roles, and your young athlete needs both. At times they need their coach to be really tough on them, while at the same time needing the understanding and encouragement from a parent. Sometimes they need a coach to be laser-focused on what they need to develop to reach their sports goal, while a parent needs to have a broader focus on developing them as people.

In my case, once my boys got really serious about their sport, they needed to hear a different voice than mine speaking into their development. Sure, I have a fair amount of knowledge of their sport and can see what they need to work on. And I still provide input to them that they listen to and try to apply—between 25% and 50% of the time! But the rest of the time, well, let's just say that they are not always attentive to my input. And when they don't listen, it eventually frustrates me. And then their eyes roll. If you have parented teenagers, you know what I'm talking about.

But for an outside coach, well, my boys don't usually grow weary of receiving instructions from them. Maybe it's that they don't think they know more than the professional coach.

The "**parent hat**" is more consequential than the "**coach hat**."

Whatever the reason, kids tend to listen more to an outside coach. And they tend to listen better, so more gets through.

And finally, while parents sometimes think we see a lot that we can help with from a coaching standpoint, usually, a skilled coach sees more. They have more training and experience, and thus more expertise to provide higher quality coaching that will help our young athletes progress faster.

There are some well-known exceptions, however. In fact, a number of high-profile parents have coached their athletes at higher levels of their sport. Steve Alford coached his son in basketball at UCLA, as did Doc Rivers in the NBA. Richard Williams coached Serena and Venus all the way to Grand Slam titles in tennis. Dabo Swinney coaches his sons in football at Clemson. And in high school sports, numerous examples are out there.

But even though some of these parent/coaches can do it at the highest levels, most experts advise against it. You see, the tension of being both a parent and a coach is real. And in extreme cases, such as the Williams sisters, the parent/coach dynamic will place significant stress on the parent/child relationship, and it could last a lifetime. Maybe you will avoid that, but is it worth taking the chance?

So, here's the advice. If you have expertise in your young athlete's sport, leverage it to help them. Speak into their development. Work with them on the side. But if at all possible, don't act as their primary coach. Hire that out. Wear your parent hat instead. It's more important and it lasts a lifetime.

11

THE PARENT IN
THE STANDS

I n the 2020 NCAA National Championship football game, the LSU Tigers were led by Heisman Trophy winner Joe Burrow. Of the 76,885 people who were in attendance that night, none got more camera time than Jimmy and Robin Burrow, Joe's parents. It is estimated that more than 26 million viewers that night watched images of the Burrow parents, at times quiet and thoughtful and at other times cheering and high-fiving the people around them exuberantly.

Most of us enjoy seeing the emotional reactions of parents in the stands because we can relate to them. We understand that watching your kids perform can be an emotional roller-coaster, full of stress, nerves, frustration and joy, to name a few of the emotions.

If you've been to many youth sports events, you've seen all

different types of behavior exhibited by parents in the stands. Below are a few of the more typical ones.

The Stoic Parent who is able to watch an entire event without displaying any hint of what they are thinking or feeling.

The Cheerleader Parent who is constantly offering encouragement to their child and teammates.

The Coach Parent (not a real coach) that frequently shouts advice and instruction from the stands.

The Negative Parent who may or may not say a word, but their young athlete is fully aware of their frustration with every mistake he/she makes.

Have you ever thought about which type you are? Or which type your young athlete would say you are? Have you ever asked them which type they want you to be?

Being a well-controlled, positive spectator is pretty easy for most parents when their kids are young and playing recreational sports. But as they progress into higher levels of competition, the investment of time and money increases, the stakes get higher, and the challenge of keeping your emotions in check becomes more difficult.

For me, this has been the toughest part of the sports parent journey. Like many of you, I LOVE watching my kids play sports, always have. I love the competition, the strategy, all of it. And my kids genuinely like having me there in the stands (at least they say they do). They seem to appreciate my interest, and they like being able to talk through their performance with me later. But while some parents seem to easily detach their emotions from what is happening on the field or court, it is challenging for me. On the outside, I strive to be 75% The Stoic Parent and 25% The Cheerleader Parent. On the inside, however, The Coach Parent and the Negative Parent battle to get out. And that internal battle can be fierce.

While many people wouldn't think I struggle with The Negative Parent (because I hide it well), I do, and my young athletes know it. For me, it's not verbal. Rather, it's a facial expression, a shrug of the shoulders or a dropping of my head at an inopportune time. It's body language, and my young athletes can read it like a book, even when no one else can. And guess what I've learned. It doesn't help them perform better. It doesn't help our relationship. And I always regret it.

I wish I could tell you that I have conquered this and share with you the secret to overcoming it once and for all. But the truth is that I will battle it again at the next tournament. Before every match, I will set my mind to positively influence my athlete's performance by conducting myself properly in the stands. I will remind myself to be encouraging at best, stoic at worst. I will pray for help and strength. And much of the time, I will win the internal battle. And when I don't, my kid will usually tell me. And eventually, I will apologize and reset once again.

When I reset, I try to remind myself that when I am in the stands, I can be a positive force to help my athlete perform and compete well, simply by the way I behave. Even in an individual sport like tennis, I can be a strong teammate that supports them and helps them succeed, just by how I conduct myself in the stands. That's a powerful idea for sports parents to embrace.

So, how do we provide that kind of support? For starters, just show up if at all possible. Showing up communicates your support, and it matters to them even if they never say it. Here's a few other ideas for you to consider.

- *Cheer and be a positive voice for your young athlete.*
- *Maintain positive body language in the stands.*
- *If it's a team sport, encourage the entire team; it is not all about your kid.*
- *Be a supporter, not a coach from the stands.*
- *Be respectful of the opponents and demonstrate great sportsmanship.*

Finally, keep in mind that when you are in the stands, you are not just another spectator to your young athlete. And you are more than just a teammate. You are their parent, one of the most important people in their lives. Remind yourself that your response from the stands can be a difference maker.

So, before the next game or match, talk to your athlete about what they need from you, what helps them the most. Reset if needed. And become the positive voice in the stands that all young athletes need. The car rides home will be better. Trust me on that.

Be a **positive** force for your athlete from the **stands**.

12

THE CAR RIDE HOME

Some time ago, I read an article about sports parenting. The author referenced a survey of hundreds of college athletes that were asked, "What is your worst memory of youth and high school athletics?" I would have expected most to answer about a very disappointing loss or a bad situation with a coach. But the overwhelming #1 response was "The car ride home with my parents." Wow! That was shocking. Or was it?

If your experience is like mine, you and your young athlete have had some great car rides home, but also some that did not go well. The ones that went well usually did so because we quickly let go of the game or match and just became parent and child again, talking about where we would eat, or anything other than what just occurred. Or maybe it went well because everything on the field or court went well, and our celebratory mood left little room for conflict.

On the other hand, the ones that did not go so well typically involved a lack of self-control on my part. For starters, my kid's performance was not their best. There were glaring improvement opportunities to discuss, things that my young athlete had neglected to work on which came home to roost, leaving us both frustrated. Yep, I usually knew it was too soon to "review the game film" on the way home, but there were times I just couldn't stop myself. Have you been there?

Early on in our sports journey, I read that parents should delay discussing what went right or wrong with their kid's performance until many hours after the competition, maybe even the next day. While this seems ideal, as a practical matter, it has been tough for me to live out at times. Really tough. After all, sometimes my young athlete wants to discuss it; they actually want to hear my opinion, and they bring it up almost immediately. And when they open the door, I have to be authentic, right?

Not so fast. If that is you, you're on dangerous ground and the next step you take is an important one. Do you want your young athlete to one day report that the worst thing about youth sports was the car ride home with you? I doubt you do. So how can you avoid it?

Let's break it down. You are a good parent who wants the best for your child, right? When you get in the car with them immediately following a challenging game or match, what do they really want from you? What do they need from you?

If you're honest, correction or advice is probably not the first thing they need. Let me illustrate.

When one of my sons was very young, he played poorly in a tournament and lost. He held his emotions together pretty well until we got in the car, when he began to cry. We talked quite a bit on the car ride home, but I didn't bring up what he did wrong on the court, nor did I mention the areas he needed to improve. Instead, I let him know he was loved and that his performance on a tennis court did not define his value as a person. I looked for ways to encourage him. And by the time we got home, his painful loss was a distant memory. In that moment, when my son was visibly hurting emotionally, I intuitively did what most parents would do, providing comfort and expressing love and acceptance.

It's pretty easy to get it right when your kids are very young. When they're older, however, they may experience the same frustration, hurt, and feelings of failure after a game or match that didn't go well. But they no longer cry. They don't seem as fragile as when they were young children. So maybe they don't need the same approach from you on the car ride home. But the truth is, they do.

They still need to learn from their failures, yes. They need to address their improvement opportunities in the days ahead. But in the immediate aftermath of a disappointing performance, they likely need the same from us that they needed when they were younger. They need the car ride to be a safe place where they can decompress. They need us to change the subject and let them know that life is more than sports. They need us to communicate that all will be fine. There will be time later to discuss what needs to be learned from the day's event. But not right now. Not in the car.

Admittedly, this is VERY challenging for many sports parents, including me. We see what needs to be corrected, and we want to share it. And our young athletes may need to hear it. But timing is critical, so we must control our tongues. And by the way, controlling your tongue by not saying ANYTHING doesn't work either, because your silence actually speaks loudly. I know because my son has told me.

So, let's do our best as parents to make the car ride home a positive experience and not a negative one. If you're like me, you won't get it right all the time, so when you mess up, 'fess up. Ask your young athlete to forgive you and try harder the next time. Your youth sports journey will be better. Your young athlete's experience will be better. And your car rides home will be memorable, for all the right reasons.

What you **say** in the car may leave a **scar**. Choose wisely.

13

SPECIALIZATION— GOING ALL IN ON ONE SPORT

While youth sports is supposed to be fun, it's also serious business. Competition is serious. Training is serious. Financial commitment is serious. Thirty years ago, most serious athletes played multiple sports, depending on whatever season was going on. Today's serious athletes often "specialize" during their teenage years, playing one sport all year.

Parents and their young athletes make the decision to specialize in spite of numerous studies that point to a variety of negative outcomes from youth sports specialization. So why do we do it?

Simply put, if your young athlete aspires to be elite, to play a sport in college or possibly even at the high school varsity level, they are competing with other young athletes that are striving to achieve the same. And since many of their competitors are working 10-12 months a year developing their skills in a single sport, specializing, splitting time between multiple sports puts them at a disadvantage.

Thus, the dilemma for parents and their athletes is created. How do we ignore the potential downsides of sports specialization? And how do our young athletes achieve their goals without embracing it?

One of my close friends is a high school athletic director who has six kids. His youngest son is a gifted athlete who is passionate about sports. In middle school, he played basketball, baseball and football, enjoying success in each. As he entered high school, he set a goal to play college baseball. And while he wanted to continue playing multiple sports, he realized that achieving his goal would require a greater commitment to one. After all, the people he was competing against were playing baseball all year. They were already specializing, and so must he. His dad is aware they will have to manage his son's training with caution, knowing that too many swings or throws could lead to injuries or burnout. At the same time, training too little will jeopardize his son's chances to achieve his sports goal.

There are exceptions to this of course. Some "cream of the crop" athletes, those gifted with exceptional talent, can sometimes achieve elite status in multiple sports. This typically occurs when one of the sports is football, which usually doesn't run on a 10-12 month cycle at the youth and high school level. But for many sports, if a teenage athlete is not training 10-12 months a year, they will struggle to keep up with their peers and competitors.

Whether we like it or not, that's just a fact. It's the youth sports culture we've created, and while numerous studies highlight the dangers of specialization, it has become the new normal in many high-level youth sports.

As parents, how do we manage this tension? What do we encourage our kids to do in terms of playing multiple sports? How do we guide them? Below are a few ideas to consider . . .

Delay specialization as long as possible, at least until high school. The sooner your athlete specializes, the quicker they will arrive at a place where their sport feels like a job, increasing the potential for early burnout. If your athlete's goals are such that they can continue playing multiple sports, encourage them to do so.

Once your athlete specializes in one sport, schedule some significant breaks from training (3-4 weeks each), even if your young athlete resists. This is healthy for them physically and mentally. Their mind, emotions, and body need breaks from the grind, and so do you.

Be careful not to overtrain each week. Studies show that teenage athletes should not train more than 16 hours per week. Not only will overtraining lead to early burnout, but there is substantial data that links overtraining to injuries—especially repetitive motion injuries.

Dr. Neeru Jayanthi, Director of Sports Medicine Research and Education at Emory Healthcare, is a leading researcher and voice on youth sports specialization. In an interview with ESPN, Dr Jayanthi said, "Kids are broken by the time they go to college. I have many who will be going to play in college next year, and this whole year has been about trying to get them healthy so they can step on that doorstep as a freshman and have a chance to participate."

Playing so much that overuse injuries may occur versus not playing enough to keep up with competitors. This is the tension of specialization we parents must wrestle with.

If your young athlete has lofty sports goals, decisions about specialization are in your future. So, read a few online studies to learn more. Talk it over with your kid. And make a decision that manages the tension in the healthiest way possible for your young athlete.

When **specializing**, commit to a **healthy** approach.

14

WHEN TO JUMP INTO THE DEEP END

M ost kids don't learn to swim in the deep end of the pool. I haven't done research to validate this, but I've been around enough pools, seen enough parents teaching their kids to swim, and taught four of my own. So, I'm pretty sure that most kids begin in the baby pool or at least the shallowest area of the big pool. And only when parents think their kids are ready should they be allowed to jump into the deep end.

Youth sports should be no different. Jumping into the deep end in sports is a big deal, for you and your young athlete. For them, it means that they are fully ready to take on the work, sacrifice and commitment to achieve a lofty, sports goal they have. For you, it means the same.

I've seen kids swimming in the deep end of sports who shouldn't be there. Parents spend big money and kids invest substantial time, but they just don't belong in the deep end. They're not really ready to work hard, they don't seem to have a firm goal, or they just really don't yet have the ability to swim with the kids that belong there. Maybe they will be ready at some point, but now is too early.

So, when is the right time? How old should they be? How do we know when to truly go for it?

For most young athletes, jumping into the deep end of their sport means saying yes to one or more of the following questions:

- *Am I ready to make the commitment to play on a high-level travel ball or AAU team?*
- *Am I ready to join a high-level academy that practices almost every day?*
- *Am I ready to drop other sports and focus on my main sport year-round?*

Each of these questions represents a decision point for parents and young athletes on whether they are ready for the next level. If you are reading this book, you are either contemplating this decision or have already moved to the deep end. If you are still weighing that decision, here are some things to consider:

Does my athlete have a realistic goal in mind? The deep end of sports is expensive, time-consuming and difficult. As mentioned in a previous chapter, it will require your kid to miss out on some other activities. Therefore, be sure there is a solid goal your young athlete is trying to achieve before diving into the deep

The **deep** end is for **serious** swimmers.

end. Otherwise, encourage them to continue playing their sport for fun and hold off on the deep end.

Is my athlete mature enough? Age is not that relevant here. What you are looking for in your athlete is the maturity required for them to set a goal for themselves and commit to achieve it. For most sports, jumping into the deep end occurs in late middle school to early high school, especially in team sports. For many individual sports, however, such as gymnastics, tennis, golf, swimming, the decision point may be earlier.

Does my athlete have the ability to achieve their goal? This is a tough one, because sometimes it's difficult to determine true ability before they are in the deep end. Some kids blossom later, in terms of skill and physicality, so what looks almost impossible now, may look different several years into it. And let's face it, there are numerous stories of people overachieving as a result of locking in on a goal and really going for it. Given that, I would err on the side of giving my young athlete a chance if they were willing to work hard and go for it.

If your answers to all of these questions are a resounding yes, then your young athlete is probably ready for the deep end. Once they are in it, they (and you) may love it and want to stay until their goal is achieved. And if they don't, well, that's a topic for another chapter.

15

WHEN THEY AREN'T WORKING HARD ENOUGH

Katie Lydecky is the greatest women's swimmer of all time. She burst onto the scene in the 2012 London Olympics, winning the first of many Olympic gold medals as a 15 year-old. Lydecky is talented, yes, but she is mostly known for her unrivaled work ethic. What sets her apart is her love for practice, driven by a relentless desire to get better every time she enters the pool. Day after day, month after month, year after year.

Katie's legendary work ethic is shared by other top athletes such as Kobe Bryant, Peyton Manning, Tiger Woods, and Tim Tebow, among others. All gifted with talent, but underlying those gifts is an elite work ethic.

If your young athlete has this type of work ethic, you should count your blessings. You will likely have to help them develop in other areas, but you won't have to push and prod them to work hard to achieve their goals. For most parents, however, you will feel the need to give your young athlete a swift kick in the pants every now and then. Or maybe a lot.

You see, unlike Katie Lydecky, your kids may not love to "get in the pool" every day. Oh, they still have their lofty goal, and they love the competitions. But loving the work is a different thing. Practicing. Conditioning. Training. Eating. Hydrating. Day in, day out. It's a grind, and most kids need some pushing from time to time in order to keep it up.

To be honest, I find this area to be the most difficult aspect of sports parenting, and after many years, I still wrestle with the same questions rattling around in my head.

- *How much pushing should I have to do if they are really committed to their goal?*
- *Are my expectations too high, given that they already work harder than many of their friends?*
- *Should I give them grace and let whatever happens happen? After all, it's their goal.*
- *Should I quit paying for everything related to their sport until they demonstrate a better work ethic?*

I contemplated leaving this chapter out, because it's still a struggle for me. At times, I frustrate my young athletes by focusing more on what they don't do in lieu of recognizing how much they actually do. At other times, I give too much grace because I don't want conflict.

Grit will take you further than **talent**.

In the midst of all of it, I'm trying to teach them that high achievers pay the price. They go back to the range and hit a thousand balls after finishing a disappointing round. They stay in the gym after a poor shooting night and shoot another 500 shots. They spend extra hours in the batting cage correcting a flaw in their swing. They embrace the grind because they understand that the payoff doesn't happen without it.

We see this in every aspect of sport, and in every aspect of life. Some people call it grit, and high achievers have it. Some come by it naturally, but most have to develop it.

As parents, we can force it for a period of time, but that creates other issues and tension. Or we can encourage it, as we encourage other character traits. Or maybe we strive for a balance between the two. I wish I had the secret sauce to share with you, but I don't think it exists.

What I have discovered is that for most young athletes, grit must be developed over time, requiring a blend of their passion for achievement with real perseverance. And oh yeah, it requires some serious patience from you. You see, parents cannot force it, but we can model it, encourage it, and expect it. And when we see evidence of grit in our young athletes, we should praise it.

So, stay the course. Expose your young athletes to the famous athletes like Katie Lydecky. Ask them to define what grit looks like to achieve their goal. Expect some ups and downs but don't be afraid to nudge them toward a gritty place. The benefits will last a lifetime.

16

WHEN THEY WANT TO QUIT

In her best-selling book, *Grit*, Angela Duckworth tells the story of NFL Hall of Fame quarterback Steve Young's freshman year at Brigham Young University. Though he had been a high school star, Young found himself as the #8 quarterback on the depth chart, assigned to the "hamburger squad," a group of the least valuable team members who ran practice plays against the team's defensive line. Things were so bad that Steve, with bags packed, called his dad and told him he wanted to quit and head home. Steve's dad let him know that he could quit, but he could not return home, because he wouldn't have a quitter in his house.

Wow! Talk about tough love. I'm not sure if many of today's young parents would endorse that style of parenting. But Steve's dad knew that his son needed to develop more grit. He needed to push through something difficult, rather than taking the safe and easy way out.

So yes, his words were tough, but they made a huge difference in Steve's life. He stayed at BYU and worked himself not only into the starting quarterback position, but he also became the top college quarterback in the country by his senior year. And he might have missed it all if his dad had let him quit.

If your young athlete is on the elite level sports journey, there may be a point along the way where they contemplate quitting. Usually it will follow a series of disappointing performances or defeats which make them question whether it's all worth it.

The idea of quitting could occur if they realize their original goal is beyond their reach or doesn't appeal to them anymore. Or maybe it happens as a result of a serious injury. Or maybe their coach is making their sports experience miserable, and they just want it to end. Whatever the reason, it's common for young athletes to consider quitting at some point.

As sports parents, how should we respond? Should we let them easily move on to another interest? Or should we take a hard line, "we don't raise quitters" approach?

Well, in some situations, we shouldn't respond at all, as our young athletes may just be blowing off steam. I bet I've heard one of my kids declare he was quitting at least half a dozen times over the years. And each time, it followed a particularly disappointing defeat.

Fortunately, I learned to simply listen and be patient with him, providing 24 hours or so for him to process his frustration. In most cases, he woke up the next day and began working even harder in pursuit of his athletic goals, without a word from me. But more than once, his lingering frustration led us to decide he should take a few days or a week away from his sport before we had discussions about the future.

Sometimes our young athletes are frustrated enough to think they want to quit, when all they really need is a break. In my opinion, the key for parents is to not overreact, as the situation will often resolve itself.

But what if your athlete genuinely wants to quit, and it is not a "heat of the moment" expression? Maybe they're facing a very challenging situation, and the adversity seems too hard to overcome. That was Steve Young's situation. And like Steve's dad, I believe parents should generally encourage their young athletes to push through rather than back off. After all, resilience is a character muscle our kids need to develop, and the best way to develop resilience is to push through adversity and finish what was started.

My guess is that each of us can remember a time in our lives when we wanted to quit, but once we got to other side, we were glad we stuck it out. Share your story with your young athlete and challenge them to press on. Especially if their sport is a team sport such as baseball, volleyball, football, basketball, etc. Quitting on the team should never be taken lightly, especially in the middle of a season.

So, once again, is it ever ok to let your young athlete quit? Absolutely. It just depends on the situation. Remember my son who said he wanted to quit multiple times after tough defeats? Well, during his senior year of high school, he began to seriously contemplate quitting his sport. We talked and prayed about it for several weeks, and he was pretty sure he no longer wanted his upcoming college life to be dominated by his sport. While he had no regrets about the past, he wanted to pursue new passions in the future.

I could have given him the "quitting" speech. But he wasn't running from adversity. He wasn't taking the easy way out. On the contrary, he had shown amazing resilience over the past eight years, pushing through numerous challenges, and I am proud of him. So, we decided he would take a month or two off and see how he felt. Several months went by, and he was even more sure of his decision. His high-level youth sports journey was over, but for the right reasons. He quit, but he was not a quitter, and I told him just that.

So, remember, context is everything when having the quitting conversation. An abrupt, thoughtless response may put unnecessary relational distance between you and your young athlete. They will hesitate before sharing their feelings with you again, and you'll wish you had taken a different approach.

On the other hand, a thoughtful, patient response will not only provide a valuable teaching moment but will also build trust and connection between you. So, take time to listen to what they are really saying when they talk about quitting. Work though it with them. You won't regret it.

Quitting doesn't make one a **quitter**. Take time to **understand** the situation.

17

DON'T NEGLECT THE MENTAL SIDE OF SPORTS

My young athletes are identical twins. They play the same sport, train the same, share the same coach, and eat the same. If you saw them practice, you would see skills that seem very similar. Given all of that, it seems like they should have similar results, right? Well, not so fast. They have, in fact, experienced different results because there is one key component of sports success where they are not the same . . . the mental side.

You see, when it comes to the big stage, one of my athletes walks onto it believing he will win, while the other doubts it. One tends to focus too long on mistakes he makes on the court, while the other usually moves on easily. One competes primarily against his opponent, while the other often competes against his opponent and himself. One's mental approach is wired in one direction, and the other is wired in the other direction.

These differences have forced me to fully embrace the importance of the mental side of sports. It is often the difference in who performs to their capabilities. And it is often the difference in who wins and who loses.

But while an athlete's mental approach is one of the most important components of success, its development is mostly neglected during the key youth sports years. We invest substantial time and money in the development of physical skills such as mastering a proper jump shot, improving your launch angle, developing your serve, improving the explosiveness of your first step, perfecting your dismount, and lengthening your drive, to name a few. But when it comes to a strong mental approach, we usually just hope our young athletes come by it naturally, and some do. But for the many that don't, what do we do? How do we help them develop a strong mental approach? What tools do we turn to that can help? Will time and maturity solve the issue?

Before trying to answer these questions, let's define this topic a little more. The mental side of sports is a broad subject that primarily addresses how athletes THINK about their performance—before, during, and after. Oftentimes, when competing athletes have similar physical skills, the one who has the superior mental approach achieves more.

Let me elaborate. One powerful component of a strong mental approach is confidence, or belief. Those who possess it have a distinct advantage over those who bring doubt to the field or court. Some athletes, like one of my sons, comes by belief naturally. For others, it must be developed.

Another key mental component involves what consumes your athlete's focus during competition. When they make a mistake, are they able to easily let it go, or do they dwell on it? Is their self-talk positive or negative? The most successful athletes are usually able to leave past mistakes behind, focusing on the next throw, at bat, point, or shot. But for others, they must develop the ability to let go of the past and focus on the present.

Finally, how does your young athlete perform in the biggest and brightness moments, in "crunch time?" For some, these big moments bring out the best in their performance, but for others, well, they tend to tighten up and perform below their abilities.

Whether it is the result of nature or nurture, young athletes are usually wired on one or the other side of the equation. If your young athlete possesses a strong mental approach in their sport, congratulations. You either did some great things along the way or are just lucky (probably the latter). But for all the rest, finding a way to overcome a negative mental approach is critical to achieving their goals. So, what can a parent do to help? At the risk of oversimplifying, below are two DIY (do it yourself) paths you can take.

- *Read several books on the mental side of sports with your young athlete. A simple google search will yield numerous results, including some specific to a given sport.*

- *Go to YouTube and search on sports psychology. You will see a number of videos you and your young athlete can watch and discuss.*

I am in the fourth quarter of my youth sports parenting journey, and I have travelled the DIY (Do It Yourself) paths to mental development. I will tell you that they require some discipline, because the ideas and tools that will be presented must be embraced and worked on by your athlete in order to make a lasting change to their mental approach.

But replacing a negative mental approach with a positive one will transform your young athlete's performance, as well as their ability to enjoy their sport. So, don't delay. Don't keep investing in physical skill development while hoping that the mental side takes care of itself. The tools are easily accessible, and they'll cost you nothing but an investment of time. And it may be the key to unlocking your athlete's potential.

Inner excellence enables **outer** excellence.

18

HIRING A SPORTS PSYCHOLOGIST

What do Russell Wilson, Michael Jordan, Aaron Judge, Tom Brady and Nick Faldo have in common? They all have relied on sports psychologists to help them maximize their performance. These top athletes understand that the mental side of sports is often the key differentiator that enables winning performance. But this is not only the case for top professional athletes, as most major college athletic programs today include access to mental coaches for their athletes.

So, if the world's best athletes understand the value of a mental coach, why do we neglect it in the youth sports arena? Why do parents invest so much in hiring expert coaching to aid in the development of outer skills but leave the development of mental toughness to chance?

If I could have a "do-over" on anything I have done to help

one of my young athletes, I would have invested in sessions with a sports psychologist early on. Unfortunately, I didn't fully grasp that the development of inner excellence was just as important—maybe more—as the investment I was making in outer excellence. And once I did grasp it, I spent too long hoping we could get there on our own.

Maybe this resonates with you. Like me, maybe you think that a proper mental approach in sports is simply part of maturity or something you can help your young athlete work through and improve upon. And for some kids, this approach works just fine. They are able to handle the mental pressures, and they naturally have a positive mindset that enables them to maximize their performance.

But some of our athletes need help re-wiring the way they think about their performance, and about themselves. They need coaching to develop the right approach to self-talk. They need some tools to help them overcome disappointing results and bring confidence to their next competition. If your athlete struggles in any of these areas, a sports psychologist can help. They will provide a safe space to talk through the pressures and the mental challenges your athlete faces in their sport, providing advice and tools your athlete will benefit from. Sports psychologists can help develop confidence, toughness, and an ability to handle the big moments.

For us, it took me a few years of thinking about it before I finally took action and found a good mental coach for my athlete to talk with. It wasn't cheap, but relative to what I was spending overall on youth sports, it wasn't significant. And for my young athlete, it was a pressure release, a safe space to truly

Mental **toughness** enables maximum **performance** on the **biggest** stages.

share and discover some of the ways in which he was competing against not only his opponent but also himself. The tools he received helped him in his sport, but more importantly, they will help him in life.

So, my advice is obvious. If you think your young athlete might need some tools to help bring the right mental approach to their sport, don't delay. A handful of sessions can make a big difference. And when it does, you'll wish you had done it sooner.

Part III

SPORTS & LIFE

19

DEVELOPING GREAT SPORTSMANSHIP

Would you rather your young athlete win an MVP award for their performance or a sportsmanship award for their behavior? For many parents, that's a tough call. I mean, let's be honest. There's a lot riding on your athlete performing at a very high level, and an MVP award shows that the work has paid off. On the other hand, being recognized for outstanding sportsmanship speaks positively to the character of your child, which will serve them well long after their sports career is over.

Hmmm.

Maybe that's a tough question to answer for you, but is it really a fair question?

You see, the question assumes that you must make a choice between the two rewards, as if your young athlete can't aspire to both. But the fact is that they can, and they should. Young athletes should strive to be the best players they can be AND ALSO to exhibit great sportsmanship. They are not mutually exclusive, and as parents we should emphasize both. Not for the purposes of winning awards, but for the purpose of achieving goals and developing strong character.

Images of poor sportsmanship among professional athletes show up on social media every day. For example, basketball stars aren't satisfied to simply dunk over an opponent. Nope, the dunk highlights our kids watch often end with the dunker standing over their opponent, or getting in their face, taunting them about the "defeat" they just suffered. In football, many players aren't satisfied to make a great play; they must follow the play up by trash-talking or taunting their opponent, as if to say, "You are nothing compared to me."

Our kids consume images like these every day while watching live games or highlights on social media and SportsCenter. Do these images really influence our kids and have an impact on the youth sports culture? I think they do. Already, we increasingly see similar examples of poor sportsmanship show up regularly in college sports, and even in high school.

How do we push back on this cultural shift going on? Well, I believe it's up to those of us who are sports parents to promote and encourage high standards of sportsmanship with our young athletes. We must talk about it. We must set the bar high. We must present a higher standard from what they are seeing on Instagram.

But does it really matter? I mean, good sportsmanship is nice, but why is it really important for sports parents to emphasize it? Let's break it down.

For starters, good sportsmanship is rooted in strong character. And at its core, sportsmanship demands that a player think not just of themselves, but also acknowledge the importance of other teammates and competitors. Sportsmanship asks that players win and lose with grace, rather than kicking a defeated opponent when they are down or pouting and making excuses that take away from an opponent's victory when one loses.

I will never forget the 1996 Masters Golf Tournament, when Greg Norman lost a six-shot lead to Nick Faldo on the final day to lose by one stroke. As devastating as this loss was to him personally, Norman sincerely congratulated Faldo after the winning putt, exhibiting tremendous grace in losing. At the same moment, Faldo tempered his victory celebration, well aware of the weight of disappointment his opponent was experiencing at that moment. Millions watched as both players demonstrated amazing sportsmanship, and most viewers had a greater respect for both players as a result.

Good sportsmanship is often characterized by self-control, humility, selflessness, kindness and integrity, character traits that will serve your young athlete well in sports and in life. And contrary to what some may think, good sportsmanship has no negative impact on performance.

The truth is that some of the greatest names in every sport—Peyton Manning, Steph Curry, Clayton Kershaw, Chris Evert, Roger Federer, Mia Hamm, Alex Morgan—not only achieved greatness in their sport but are also admired for great sportsmanship in the way they competed, the way they treated their competitors, and the way they handled both victory and defeat.

Like most of you, I have witnessed many examples of good sportsmanship in youth sports, leaving me with respect and admiration for those young athletes. I have also seen numerous examples of poor sportsmanship along the way.

For some kids, the bad acts occur over and over again. For others, they are blips that present teaching moments for parents as our young athletes develop and mature. In either case, sports parents should be front and center when it comes to teaching and modeling good sportsmanship to our young athletes. Coaches should contribute, but in my opinion, parents must take the leadership role here. Remember, good sportsmanship is the residue of strong character and helping our kids develop strong character is a primary mission for parents.

So, how do we teach good sportsmanship? First, start early, as soon as your athlete begins playing a sport. Define sportsmanship for them and why it matters. And when they exhibit it, praise them for it as much as you praise a great hit, catch, basket, tackle or shot.

As they get older and the competition becomes more intense, continue to notice and emphasize great sportsmanship. And by all means, don't hesitate to address poor sportsmanship, but try not to do it in the heat of the moment. Wait until things cool down and have a discussion.

And finally, remember the old saying, "The apple doesn't fall far from the tree." It's usually true, so set the example. Don't be that parent who constantly berates the officials, treats their kid's opponent disrespectfully, or isn't a graceful winner or loser. Instead, model good sportsmanship and demonstrate the kind of character you want for your athlete. They are watching.

Great **sportsmanship** is the residue of strong **character**, **enhancing** your athlete's stature in sports and **life**.

20

OVERCOMING ADVERSITY

I have a lifelong friend whose oldest son has been an elite athlete since he was very young. While he was extremely gifted in several sports, by high school he settled on football, and the local high school varsity coach was enthusiastic about his future star quarterback. His arm was strong, his speed and athleticism were off the charts, and some were saying he was a "can't miss" NFL prospect.

Then the injuries came, one after another. Multiple concussions. Then, shoulder surgery limited his throwing ability, ending his quarterback dream. He changed positions and pressed on in his pursuit of playing football at the next level. As the injuries kept coming, many people wondered why he didn't just give up. But he didn't. He pushed through adversity over and over again, until realizing his goal of playing at a major SEC school.

In four years there, he saw limited playing time because, yep, you guessed it, the injury bug continued. But he stuck it out and graduated from that university.

He and his parents have been on quite a journey. The adversity he faced was surely discouraging at times, but he never let it defeat him. On the contrary, his inner strength, bolstered by his strong faith, have shaped him in a way that will show up big in his future. In fact, he is just beginning his "adult life," and as we all know, he will encounter more adversity along the way. But he will be ready to handle it, thanks to the character he developed through sports.

Adversity shows up in many forms along the youth sports journey, and chances are your young athlete will experience it in one form or another. It may appear as a coach that doesn't provide them a fair chance to show what they can do. It may show up as an injury or other physical limitation. Adversity may show up as a mental struggle that causes an athlete to underperform on the big stage over and over again. Or maybe it's a financial hardship that limits access to higher level training or coaching that others are getting.

Simply put, adversity is anything that stands in the way of your young athlete accomplishing their goal. It is a wall to get over, a barrier to break through, or a burden to overcome. All athletes experience it in one form or another. For the fortunate ones, the adversity they face is relatively easy to overcome, and they move through it quickly. For others, adversity seems to appear over and over, in many different forms, testing their desire and resolve.

Adversity builds **character** when responded to correctly.

If your young athlete is in this camp, buckle up. Their journey, and yours, will be a challenging one, full of ups and downs. They may or may not achieve their sports goal, but with your help, they can develop something much greater, a character trait that will serve them well throughout life.

The character trait I'm referring to is resilience. Some refer to it as endurance. Whatever you call it, it's the ability to push on when things get really hard, to bounce back when you get knocked down. Developing the resilience muscle is not a process we look forward to, nor do our athletes appreciate it while it is happening. But they will later. They will need it to achieve their sports goal, and they will need it later in life.

Youth sports is certainly not the only place to develop resilience, but for most young athletes, the opportunity will present itself. As parents, you will need to help them recognize it. You will need to encourage perseverance, endurance and toughness, praising their strength and resolve. You will need to set aside your own frustration and provide them with an empathetic ear. You will need to have a longer perspective, understanding the value of the character trait they are developing, even when their sports goal is threatened.

Ultimately, your young athlete will have to push through, mentally and physically. They will have to press on to overcome the challenge. And when they do, they will be rewarded with something of incredible value to call on later in life. Probably numerous times. This is the hidden value of the youth sports journey, the unexpected return on investment.

21

LEADERSHIP DEVELOPMENT IN SPORTS

I recently did a search on Amazon for books on leadership and guess what I found. Twenty pages of leadership books! I'm guessing there are many more, but Amazon cut off the search at twenty pages.

Why so many?

Well, probably because there is an insatiable hunger in our culture for developing leaders. From books to conferences to podcasts, there is an ocean of opportunities to learn about leadership.

And let's be honest; we all want our kids to become leaders, don't we? But is that really possible, or are some kids pre-wired to become leaders and others to be followers? Or can everyone develop leadership skills and grow into an effective leader?

I believe they can. And more importantly, many leadership experts believe the same.

You see, leadership is not about the position you hold. It's not about having the most powerful voice on the team. In fact, I would bet we've all been in situations where the boss, the captain, or the senior person on your team wasn't a good leader at all. On the flip side, we've all experienced or watched teams in which the true leaders were not the highest profile people.

Why? Because simply put, leadership is defined by influence, rather than by position.

The true leaders among us are those that leverage their words and/or their actions to influence those around them. And thus, the ability to influence, rather than be influenced, is the measure of true leadership. And that's the kind most parents want their kids to develop.

So, what does this have to do with youth sports?

Well, if you want your son or daughter to develop leadership abilities, there is no better place to begin than in the world of youth sports. Don't believe me? Well, numerous studies confirm it.

One such study, conducted by Human Kinetics in 2017, looked at how athletic participation and other factors affect students' leadership skills. Student-athletes scored significantly higher than non-athletes in overall transformational leadership. "Participation in sport builds confidence and character in high-pressure situations. Student athletes needed to manage change and failure on a continuous competitive basis. They needed to encourage and influence team members to pursue team goals," the study's authors wrote.

Another study published in the *Journal of Leadership & Organizational Studies* in 2014 found that varsity-level high school athletes "appeared to demonstrate higher levels of leadership and had higher-status careers."

I could go on and on referencing studies that confirm the leadership development opportunities that student athletes enjoy. For example, team sports provide opportunities for athletes to learn how to influence teammates, put team goals ahead of their own, hold others accountable, and be accountable themselves. Team sports also create opportunities for young athletes to learn how to manage conflict, listen to their teammates, and make themselves heard.

In addition, athletes in both individual and team sports learn to think strategically, to shift to Plan B when Plan A isn't working. They also have great opportunities to learn how to overcome adversity, to work hard in pursuit of a goal, and to demonstrate integrity in their sport.

Finally, since most young athletes have experienced both good and bad coaching—and lots of it—along their journey, they often are far ahead of others when it comes to understanding how best to motivate and influence others.

Now, I want to stress something very important. I've used the word "opportunity" numerous times in this chapter, and that was intentional. You see, young athletes are not assured of developing these leadership skills and qualities. Some will happen naturally, but others won't. But the opportunities will be there.

As sports parents, this is where we come in. And once again, it requires intentionality. For example, if your young athlete is more of an introvert, encourage them to develop and use their voice with their teammates. Share a few ideas with them on how to be an influencer. Talk to them about becoming a problem solver on the field or court.

Above all, seize the opportunities to encourage development of these critical leadership skills. Offer praise when you see them in your young athlete. Be on the lookout for teachable moments to reinforce their importance. More than hitting, throwing, dribbling, kicking or serving a ball, these skills will serve them well. For a lifetime.

Leadership is **influence**. You don't have to be the best player to be a **leader**.

22

RELIEVE
THE PRESSURE

Today's teenagers are stressed out, and the statistics confirm it. More than 20% are suffering from some form of depression. Suicide is now the third leading cause of death for teens. Substance abuse is rampant.

Experts point to a wide array of "causes" for these alarming trends, but one thing we all know is that today's teens face significant pressure to perform at a high level. Academic pressure. Social pressure. And while sports can provide an outlet for our kids to enjoy, elite-level sports can actually increase the pressure on our young athletes even more.

Am I progressing towards achieving my goal? Am I performing as well as, or better than, my competitors? Am I meeting the expectations of my coach? Am I meeting

PARENTING THE PURE ATHLETE

*the expectations of my parents? What happens if I don't
reach my goal?*

These are only some of the thoughts our young athletes
wrestle with, and they all add pressure.

As a sports parent, we have substantial power to increase
or relieve the stress our kids are feeling, simply in the way we
interact with them. The most powerful of these shows up in
our conversations, and when they are focused too much on
sports, we may be unintentionally turning up the heat.

If you are like me, this is challenging. You see, I love sports
AND I love my kids. Put those two things together, and it is
easy for me to place too much emphasis on their sports goals,
and subsequently talk about it too much. It's also easy for me
to justify that it's ok when I do. After all, I am spending a lot
of money, time, and energy to help them achieve their dreams.
And most of the time, my athletes like to talk about it too.

Until it becomes too much.

So, how do we know when the conversations we have with
our young athletes are out of balance? For me, there are usually
some strong indicators. The first is my wife, who thankfully
doesn't hesitate to point out to me when I need to change the
conversation. In the moment, I don't always love that advice,
even though I need to hear it.

When she isn't around, it's still fairly easy to recognize
when I'm talking too much about my kid's sport, if I'm paying attention. Our conversation will eventually become pretty
one-sided, and I'm on the side that is doing most of the talking.
My athlete looks at his phone, or gives me the blank stare, or

Change the conversation, reduce the **pressure**.

gives me single word answers, all of which let me know he isn't engaged.

Sometimes I'm oblivious and keep right on talking about their sport. At best, I'm wasting my words. At worst, my over-emphasis on their sport is adding pressure. And here's the ironic part. For most young athletes, increased pressure does not produce better performance.

Like many of you, I'm still learning. I don't always get it right, but I desire to support my kids in a manner that enables them to achieve without pressuring them to achieve. And one of the easiest ways to do that is to manage our conversations away from their stress points.

Not always though. It's important that we communicate about such an important area of their lives. But there is more to their lives than sports. So, let's change the conversation, reduce the emphasis and thus, relieve the pressure.

23

WORKING THROUGH YOUR OWN DISAPPOINTMENT

My son was hobbling to the car with a huge ice wrap on his right knee. He had just spent 30 minutes with the tournament trainer being evaluated and having the ice wrap applied. He was quiet, processing what had just taken place.

It was the summer before his senior year, an important time to build his recruiting resume and impress college coaches. He had only returned to competition a few months earlier, having spent five months rehabbing after surgery on his left knee. That surgery followed a rehab program from another injury that had kept him out of competition for nine months. In each of these cases, he had worked extremely hard to get back. Doctor visits. MRIs. Many trips to the physical therapist. And on and on for months until he was ready to go. Then, repeat.

To his credit, he never gave up. He worked hard to catch up to his competitors. And here he was in a big tournament, playing well and progressing through the draw. And then it happened. In the first game of a match he expected to win, he took an unspectacular step and the right knee buckled. Immediately, we both knew it was over. Again.

Like him, I was quiet as we began the long car ride home. Like him, I was extremely disappointed. I'm not proud of my silence but this injury felt like a gut punch, and I needed time to process it. My silence caused him to wonder if I was disappointed in him and a conversation ensued. "My disappointment is for you, not because of you," I assured him. Then, with much effort, I pushed my own disappointment aside and tried to encourage him, letting him know that he could still achieve his dream.

`If your kid is pursuing an elite-level sports goal, disappointment is inevitable. The strongest and weakest performers alike will all experience it at some level. Disappointment from a loss. Disappointment from a coach not believing in them. Disappointment from an injury. Disappointment from the realization that a long-pursued goal might not be achieved. For some, it will be short-lived; for others, disappointment will be a capstone to their youth sports experience.

And that's just the kids.

We don't talk about it much, but if you are a sports parent, you will deal with some of these same disappointing experiences. And in fact, sometimes it's more difficult to handle what is happening to your kid rather than to you. Sometimes we are so invested in the hopes and dreams of our young athletes, both physically and emotionally, that the disappointing experiences are just as difficult for parents.

But we can't really afford to show disappointment, can we? Our young athletes need us to help them move through their disappointment, to stuff our own feelings as we try to lift their spirits, right?

I'm going to go out on a limb here and say that while I think that's right MOST of the time, I don't think it's right ALL the time. Some will disagree with me and that's okay. But I think there are times when it's healthy for parents to be authentic about our own disappointment. I think it's ok to be bummed *with* your athlete about a loss, or a coach's decision that negatively impacted them, or even an injury. It's good to be real. Just keep a few key things in mind.

First, the disappointment you display should be less than your athlete's, and you should move beyond it fairly quickly, looking ahead to what comes next on the journey. This may be challenging at times, but our kids look to us for stability and assurance about the future, especially in response to disappointment. We need to model to them how to process disappointment in a healthy way, even in an athletic context.

Next, and most importantly, take great care in letting them know you are disappointed WITH them, not IN them. This is a key distinction and don't assume they know it. Often they don't, and they will assume that if you are disappointed in something related to their sport, they caused it. And that only compounds their own disappointment.

That begs the question. Can you ever be disappointed IN them? You bet, but not for losing or playing poorly or even underachieving. That happens to everyone in sports.

As good sports parents, we should only be disappointed IN our young athletes for one of three things . . . poor attitude, poor behavior (including disrespecting an opponent or official), or lack of effort. To me, these are character issues, and my young athletes know that I will be very disappointed IN them should any of these occur. And if or when they do, consequences follow.

So, if you are just beginning the journey into high-level sports parenting, expect some disappointments along the road. For your young athlete, and probably for you. Come alongside them, by all means. But don't pile your disappointment on top of theirs. Instead, move through it and help them do the same.

Be disappointed **with** them.
Be disappointed **for** them.
But avoid being
disappointed **in** them.

24

SEIZING THE RELATIONAL OPPORTUNITY

It's not that difficult to find stories that highlight the strain that youth sports can place on a parent's relationship with their athlete. Numerous professional athletes have shared their own stories of the pressure, demands, and expectations that ultimately led to estrangement.

But what about the other stories? The good ones. The ones which produced great weekends and wonderful memories. The ones when relationships grew.

I can't tell you how many long dinners my boys and I have had at various sports bars throughout the Southeastern states watching the Atlanta Braves, college football or some other sporting event together after a full day of competition. I love those memories.

My guess is that many sports parents have similar stories. And you can too.

The good stories I'm referring to are not perfect ones. Every interaction is not bliss. There will be bumps on the road. There will be unexpected detours and challenges to overcome. There will be tension to work through, you can be sure, but that's true of every good story.

So, when you get to the end of the journey, how do you ensure that your relationship with your young athlete is better for it? Maybe it will just happen. For some, it does. But do you want to roll the dice on it? Or would you rather bring some intentionality to the table, increasing your odds of landing in the group that has a great story? If you're reading this chapter, I'm guessing you would.

Here's the good news. If you're on the high-level youth sports journey with your kid, you are already investing the most important component of a growing relationship . . . TIME. Lots of it. Windshield time going back and forth to practice multiple days per week. Time traveling to games or matches. Time in restaurants. Time at hotels. Time at home discussing plans. Any parent who has taken the youth sports journey will validate the substantial quantity of time required.

And that's your opportunity. It's right in front of you.

So, what are you doing with that time? Are you just a chauffeur, or are you using the time in the car to build relationship? Is the restaurant simply a place to refuel and the hotel just a

Youth sports will **end**.
Relationships last **forever**.

place to rest? Or are you leveraging these amazing opportunities to share quality time with your son or daughter?

Author Stephen Covey once said, "The key is in not spending time, but in investing it." Is the time you are giving as a sports parent an expense or an investment? Are you investing this time wisely, with intentionality? If you're reading this and realize you've been spending instead of investing, it's not too late to modify your approach; to turn the remaining *quantity* of time with your athlete into *quality* time.

One word of caution. Don't go overboard trying to squeeze something positive out of every minute. It's okay to jump on your laptop while they play a video game, or to listen to a podcast in the car while they text with friends. You don't have to go from 10% engagement to 90%. Just simply look to increase the engagement level you currently have with your young athlete.

Talk about their sport, yes, but also talk about life. Watch something together. Listen to a podcast you're both interested in while driving—then talk about it. It's not that difficult, but it requires intention. It requires time, and you have it.

So, invest it in the relationship. Seize the opportunity. When the journey is over, you'll be glad you did.

25

THE LIKELY
END GAME

Michael Jordan was cut from his high school basketball team. You've probably heard the story, even though it isn't entirely accurate. Michael was never cut, rather, he was "left off" the varsity team as a 5'10" sophomore at Laney High School, even though his fellow sophomore, 6'7" Leroy Smith, made the team. Michael went home that night and cried. But his parents raised him to push through the disappointment, and he did. In fact, he starred that year on the JV team before starring on the varsity team the following two years.

You know the rest of the story. National championship at the University of North Carolina. Six NBA championship rings. He is widely regarded as the greatest basketball player of all time, the GOAT. From high-level youth athletics to a legendary pro career. What a story. Sounds great, right? But your young athlete's story, and mine, will likely not end like this. Not even close.

Sorry if that's a downer, but just being real. Statistics show that only 7% of high school athletes play in college, less than 2% playing NCAA Division 1. And only a small percentage of those play professionally.

Those are the facts. Maybe your athlete will make it, if that's their goal. But most don't.

For the ones that don't play professionally or in college, they will finish their youth sports journey either very satisfied or disappointed. The satisfied ones never planned to play beyond high school or decided at some point to let go of their goal of playing college ball. Others fall short of their goal to play on the varsity team in high school or maybe miss out on their dream of playing in college, and thus experience disappointment.

In either case, the youth sports chapter of their story is over, and the page turns to the next chapter of life. Once again, this is true for 93% of all high school athletes, so if it happens to yours, they are part of a BIG club.

For most young athletes, the turning of the page is not traumatic. Whether they pushed hard all the way to the finish line or tapped out early, most transition out of the high-level sports grind pretty easily. They embrace new interests to fill the large blocks of open time on their schedule. They have more time to expand their social life. They begin the college adventure and enjoy playing intramural or club sports. In short, they get on with life.

And from what I've observed, most don't regret the youth sports journey they travelled.

The journey is short. **Savor** it.

As for the sports parents, the adjustment is bittersweet for many. They are weary from the grind and it feels good to step away. They may feel relieved to put a halt to the considerable expenses. Many are happy to have their weekends back.

You may feel the same way one day. But if you are like many parents I've talked to, you will miss parts of it. The competition. The friendships. The excitement. The thrill of victory (sorry, you won't miss the agony of defeat). The quality time with your young athlete.

I am in the last year of my journey. One son has already left the arena. The other is still pursuing his goal of playing in college, so we are still after it. But the end is near. At times I dread it. At times I can't wait. Either way, I have no regrets. And so far, neither do my kids.

The end will come sooner than you think. Your athlete may reach their original goal, but if they don't, all is not lost. Because the value is not only found in achieving the goal. No, the greater value is found all throughout the journey. Make it a great one.

27

IS IT WORTH IT?

One day, the final whistle will blow. The buzzer will sound. The last hole will be played. The final out is made. The last handshake is given. The end of your youth sports journey has arrived.

Upon crossing the finish line, some of you won't look back. You won't spend a lot of time thinking about the youth sports journey you were on. Instead, you're on to the next chapter of life, and the busyness just takes another form.

For others, and for me, we are more inclined to evaluate the journey we just completed, in light of all we put into it. We will remember many of the experiences, both the fun and the challenging ones. We may look back and ponder the significant investment of time and money, in comparison to the benefits we and our young athletes received. And for those of us who reflect, we are presented with a simple question—was it all worth it?

For those of you closer to the start of the journey, your question is similar as you anticipate the road ahead—will it be worth it?

Before writing this chapter, I reached out to a dozen or so parents who have completed the youth sports journey with their young athletes. All have different stories. Their kids played football, baseball, basketball, tennis, soccer, golf, track, cross country and volleyball. Some of their kids went on to play in college, while others ended their journey when they graduated from high school. What they all had in common though, was a substantial investment of time and money in the youth sports journey.

I asked each of them the following two questions.

Looking back at your journey . . .

1. *Was it all worth it?*
2. *Why or why not?*

The overwhelming response to the first question was a resounding YES! And as I read their answers to the follow-up question, I learned why.

It wasn't the scholarship money, because most of their athletes received none. And for those that did, in only one case did it make up for the amount their parents spent on youth sports development.

What I did hear back from them were some of the ideas discussed in the chapters of this book. In fact, what made it all worth it for most of these parents was the personal development that youth sports produced in their young athletes.

You bet it's been **worth** it, and I would do it all over **again**.

They pointed to the development of character traits that would serve their kids well throughout life. They pointed to how their kids had learned to be purposeful in their pursuit of important goals. And they pointed to the relational time they enjoyed with their young athletes that may have been missed if not for the youth sports journey.

Character. Life skills. Relationships.

The parents I surveyed all realized and valued these benefits. The same is true for me. And it can be true for you. And I'm betting that when your time comes, you will answer the questions the same way I do . . .

Epilogue:

THE FINAL RESULT— A PURE ATHLETE

I know, I know. I waited until the end to reference the title of the book. Maybe not the smartest approach, but I think it's easier to understand the concept of a Pure Athlete after reading the rest of the book.

You see, I believe a Pure Athlete is one that adopts a total person development approach to sports that also prepares them for life. This approach does not guarantee a pro career, or even a college scholarship. But it does enable young athletes to maximize their performance potential on the field, court, track, pool, or course. It helps them to become the best athlete they can be.

More importantly, the Pure Athlete approach will help your athlete become better at life, equipping them with the tools, disciplines and character to achieve success in all areas of life.

Let me elaborate a bit more about the Pure Athlete model.

- First, Pure Athletes have a **vision** for what they want to achieve. They have learned how to maintain focus on their desired destination, while breaking it down into achievable, time-based goals both in sports and in life.
- Pure Athletes learn and apply the value of **grit**; demonstrating perseverance and resilience when things are good and when the going gets tough. In sports and life.
- Pure Athletes are committed to developing their **skills** to a high level, leveraging intentional practice and welcoming expert coaching throughout both their sports and life journeys.
- Pure Athletes **believe** they can achieve big things; they have learned the importance of mental toughness, performance under pressure, and the positivity and resolve to turn short-term defeat into long-term victory.
- And finally, Pure Athletes are people of strong **character**. They leverage sports to learn the value of teamwork, and they understand how to lead, influence, and serve others in order to achieve a common goal. These traits, along with the sportsmanship lessons they learn in youth sports serve them well across all facets of life.

Vision. Grit. Skills. Belief. Character.

These are the pillars of the Pure Athlete model; the success factors to help our young athletes maximize performance in sports and in life.

So, rethink your sports parenting goals if needed. Strive to ensure that your athlete develops the tools and abilities to succeed not only as a young athlete, but also as adults in their careers, marriages, and parenthood.

Help them to become a Pure Athlete, ready to achieve all their goals!

PUREATHLETE™

Pure Athlete's mission is to help young athletes develop into the best versions of themselves, both in sports and in life. To that end, we provide athletes, parents, and coaches with relevant information and resources to enhance all aspects of their sports development, regardless of the sport. We also share powerful, compelling youth development stories from notable athletes across the sports spectrum to inform and inspire young athletes, parents, and coaches.

To learn more about Pure Athlete
and join our community,
please engage with us:

www.pureathleteinc.com

Acknowledgments

The writing of this book has been an amazing experience of reliving numerous youth sports experiences and contemplating the many parenting truths and principles I learned—often the hard way—throughout the journey. There are a number of people who have contributed to making this book possible, offering encouragement, feedback, collaboration and guidance along the way, and I owe them my heartfelt thanks and recognition.

First, I want to thank my twin boys, Brittain and Jack, for allowing me to share their stories, the good and the bad, without hesitation. I loved making this journey with you, and I so appreciate your willingness to forgive me and quickly overcome the rough patches when I let the challenges of the journey get the best of me. The biggest wins of our journey for me were the many times other parents made positive comments regarding your character.

Next, I want to thank Annie and Katherine, my two older daughters, whose broad array of interests—music, drama, sports, movies, eating/hanging out helped keep me balanced (somewhat). Watching you two grow and mature has taught me that seeing your child discover and enjoy their gifts is an awesome thing, regardless of what those gifts or passions are. You've both become amazing young women and I couldn't be prouder.

I could never have written this book without the collaboration and encouragement from my wife and best friend, Kay. Her willingness to read each chapter, always sharing her thoughts in an encouraging manner helped me get to the finish line on this venture. More importantly, I'll forever be grateful to her for always challenging me to keep the main thing— parenting well—the main thing along our sports journey.

In addition, I want to thank my sister, Cathy, for believing in this project and showing consistent interest, support, and encouragement. And thanks to my Mom and Dad for always supporting me in all I do.

I also owe a lot to a number of close friends. Brad Williams— thanks so much for the vast number of lunch conversations we had about sports parenting. Many of the good decisions I made along the way resulted from those conversations. I'm also thankful to Brad and another one of my closest friends, John Kimmel. You two were the first non-family members to read this book and provide feedback, within days of when I sent you the manuscript. Your positivity and belief put wind in my sails, and I am truly grateful. I also want to thank Evan McLaughlin for all your support, especially for your design skills in creating the cover and quote pages art for the book. In addition, I want to thank Bill and Terri Willits, Dana McArthur and Gary Neibur for your encouragement throughout this process.

I also want to thank two important coaches that my boys and I were privileged to share parts of our journey with. I will forever be grateful to Aubrey Jackson, who began coaching Brittain and Jack at 10 years old. Aubrey continues to provide help whenever we ask. Aubrey was a strong mentor and positive influence on them beyond tennis, and he was a confidante and sounding board for me. I will forever be grateful to Aubrey and his contribution to so much of what shows up on the pages of this book.

The second coach I want to thank is Todd Hedden, the coach of their high school tennis team. Thanks for all the "off the court" help you have provided my boys throughout their high school experience, and for making their high school tennis TEAM experience one of the best parts of their youth sports journey. And, thank you so much for your professional expertise in helping edit the content of this book.

Last, but certainly not least, I want to thank Katherine Lloyd, not only for your help designing the interior pages of the book, but also for the expertise and guidance you provided this first-time author along the way.

About the Author

Britt Lee is the co-founder of Pure Athlete, Inc. and *Parenting the Pure Athlete* is his first book, born out of his passion for youth sports—as a participant and parent—and its potential impact on kids and families.

Britt spent the first 20 years of his career in various marketing and executive leadership roles with a Fortune 500 company before starting his own marketing and brand consulting business in 2007.

Britt received his undergraduate degree from the Georgia Institute of Technology, and later earned his M.B.A. from Georgia State University.

Britt and his wife Kay live in Johns Creek, Georgia and have four kids. His daughters are both recent college graduates and his twin sons began college in 2021. He and his wife are founding members of North Point Community Church, where he served as an elder. Britt also serves on the board of Smiley For Kylie, a charitable organization committed to the cure of childhood cancer.

Made in United States
Orlando, FL
13 February 2024

43634620R00088